A
FAMILY TREE

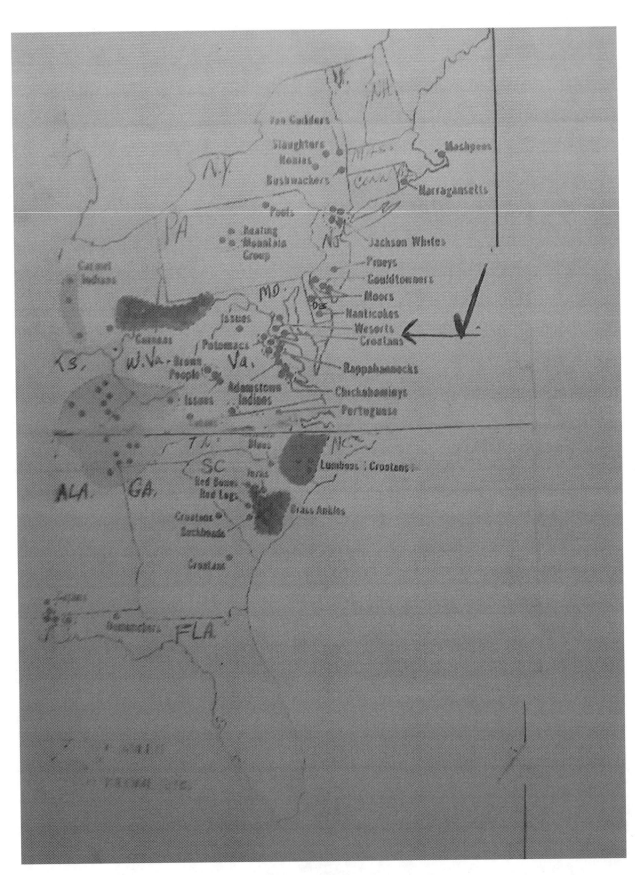

CLOSE-UP MAP SHOWING LOCATION OF WESORTS.

WESORT-MULATTO-INDIANS

(AN ETHNIC TRI-RACIAL ISOLATE GROUP)
OF
PORT TOBACCO AND LA PLATA, MARYLAND

The
"MULINDIAN NATION"

"Miss Utera"

authorHOUSE

AuthorHouse™
1663 Liberty Drive
Bloomington, IN 47403
www.authorhouse.com
Phone: 1 (800) 839-8640

Published by AuthorHouse 08/29/2018

ISBN: 978-1-5462-3284-1 (sc)
ISBN: 978-1-5462-3283-4 (e)

Library of Congress Control Number: 2018907433

Print information available on the last page.

Any people depicted in stock imagery provided by Getty Images are models,
and such images are being used for illustrative purposes only.
Certain stock imagery © Getty Images.

This book is printed on acid-free paper.

A "Map" of Ethnic Racial Isolate Groups of Partial Indian Origins

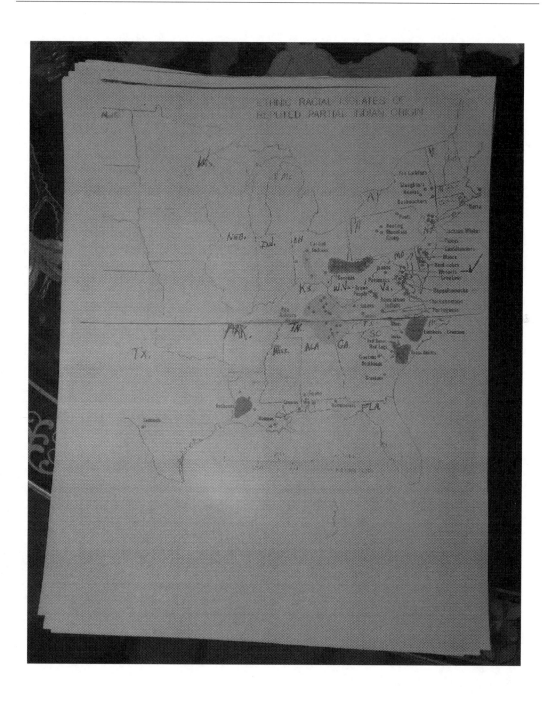

Dedication

****

This book is written <u>in memory of</u> my father, <u>Charles Wm. Cook</u>, and <u>in dedication</u> to his first-cousin, <u>Agatha Proctor King</u> who lives in Washington, DC. Without the wealth of information provided by my "Aunt Aggie", this book would never have been written. One million "Obrigadas"* to my aunt, "Aggie", from <u>Carmenlita Uter Cook</u> who writes under her legal pen-name, <u>"Miss Utera".</u>

****

*"Obrigada" means "Thank you." In Portuguese.

Introduction

This book, the "Wesort-Mulatto-Indians", aka *the "Mulindian Nation"*, was written to pay *equal homage* to the author's grandmother, = her very light, nearly-white paternal grandmother, Sarah Proctor, and also written as a parallel to her first book entitled *the "Geechee-Lady"*, which was written in honor of her very dark-skinned, maternal grandmother, Bessie.

"Grandma-Bessie" had entered the world among her people in an impoverished, and tightly-knit community of poor residents who were a mixture of *the survivors of the humble, oppressed, & persecuted Cherokee Indians*, crammed together with the downtrodden and abused, black ex-slaves,....(*as they were within one small island-community*), were a decidedly 'countrified' and patwa-sounding / gullah- speaking, non-privileged class of ("uss") = *unified-subjugated-souls* known as the full-Black and part-Cherokee *"Geechees";* = the very first inhabitants of the exotic & tropical Sea Islands located off the coast of South Carolina & Georgia, at the mouth of the Ogeechee River.

Sidebar:

A "psychological-insight" into the *private & secretive mind-sets* of light-skinned, bronze-toned people who, *(while although classified by society under the treasured, yet somewhat caustic term,"light-skinned")*,... are still not "nearly-white-enough", and therefore virtually "powerless". Among this type are found many persons who constantly find themselves living somewhat dichotomous, mentally-torn existences,...because at the mere idea of having to identify oneself by actually "choosing" an ethnic/racial group on a governmental document, many of them become flustered, confused, and sometimes, "freaked out" about the lack of proper governmental recognition or representation, and the insult of being tossed around by one's own government like highly-strung ping-pong balls, that are left to fly through the air and **to land at some unknown identity-spot, whilst other citizens know exactly which box to check on those census forms.**

It is an insult and an embarrassment, because while although known to be wrapped up into such admirable and golden, sun-kissed, "mulatto-hues",...they are, *(they know)*, still being *subtly disrespected* and **deemed by the United States government as owners of nondescript, non-recognized identity spots, and just thrown aside, to be located somewhere out in the stratosphere, which is really nowhere, not being really black, nor really white,...but classified as a "Wesort", or as a "tri-racial-isolate"; a category which has shown up only one time on a governmental form, when the term, WESORT was actually FINALLY included on the list of ethnic/racial categories on the year, 2000 Federal Census.**

However, to be classified under **this little-known ethnic category, "Wesort"**, is exactly the same as being **stuck "smack-jammed" in the middle** of the old-school **"colorism" of the "Baby-Boomers" (born 1944 to 1964),** and the ongoing skin-tone wars of nowadays' **"X-Generation"; millennials born 1965 to 1985.**

My father, Charles Cook and his first-cousin Agatha Proctor, were born into the middle of the USA-of-America's style of a caste-system known simply as "people "being-color-struck", but better-known today, simply as "colorism". Colorism is a natural 'by-product' of racism rooted in "white-supremacy". Therefore, when racism disappears, so will colorism.

But, another great solution to colorism would be for the United States government to finally give proper recognition to the "Ethnic Tri-racial Isolates of Partial Indian Origins".

"Voice of a Wesort/Creole Woman'
by "Miss Utera"

Part of me is from the slave, and the other part is
from _the master._
Part of me is black as coal, while the other part is as white
as alabaster.

Part of my hair is "krinkly",…and the other part is _Indian-straight,_
While still another part is sort-of-wavy, on 'count of being sort-a _intermediate;_
'cause I suppose, like me, , sometimes that hair just wants to be "sassy',
while the other part wants to be _sedate._

Part of me loves _"rhythm & blues",_ while the other part loves
"classica".
Part of me loves home-fried fish, but the other part prefers
caviar.

Part of me loves the sun,… but the other part loves the rain.
Part of me loves "sweet sugar-cane juice***and the other loves
champagne.

Part of me loves men whom are Black, the other part loves men whom
are White.
Both types have given me lots of love;
And both types have given me lots of strife.

***Rum is made from sugar-cane.

Those USA-citizens born in years that precede the *"Baby-Boomers"*, (= born prior to 1944), are called **"the Silent Generation"**,

Just by going online to **YouTube,** and simply typing in the term, "colorism", and/or by typing in the new jargon "team-dark-skin and team-light-skin", you will find yourselves besieged and overwhelmed by "Skin-Tone Wars" among YouTuber subscribers and random commenters!

As a "baby-boomer", I, *(Miss Utera),* find myself culturally-shocked by the ideas of "the new-millennial/"X-generation", who literally are known to implement separation of teams utilizing skin-tone terminology. I thought that during the civil-rights era of the 60s, we, *the people-of-color of my 'boomer generation'* had made very progressive strides to wipe out "colorism" as a part of the civil-rights movement.

However, the "new millennials" are proving me wrong because problems still exist!

For me, a "boomer", it is like being a dual citizen, "stuck" mid-stream between two very different & strong posts on two opposing military bases; one foreign & the other domestic, with the fear of not wanting to become a "member" of either team, because no matter which side I choose, *I would be taking sides with the enemy since I identify very strongly with both sides.*

How could I ever do such a thing, knowing very well that both of those "team-spots" were, "back-in-the-days", undeniably and staunchly owned with confidence and conviction by people who looked almost exactly like my two (2) very own, very different and divergent grandmothers; and knowing this, how could I ever take either side, knowing that I come from strong representatives of both sides, with one grandmother being nearly "jet-black" named "Bessie", and the other one, being "nearly-snow-white", named "Sarah".

In distinct contrast to "grandma-Bessie", *the "Geechee Lady", who was born in 1888, on a little South Carolina sea-island among the humble descendants of the Cherokee "Trail of Tears" survivors, crammed together with the descendants of black-slaves into one little, down-trodden-island-community),........* **grandmother-Sarah, a "Wesort-Mulatto-Indian",... (was born one year after Bessie in 1889, in the somewhat more up-to-date, southern city of La Plata).**

Sarah Proctor came into the world among her people, the genteel, colored-elite; ...an intermediate color-caste, who were the "free-people-of-color" of southeast Port Tobacco & La Plata, Maryland,... people known as the proud, self-sufficient, well- educated, softly-spoken, well-mannered, very well-dressed, and always smoothly- coiffured, so-called "good-haired" & light-skinned "Wesorts".

- It was during an era when **RACISM was "KING";** a stark-white, ruthless & headless monarch that ranted, ruled, and raged throughout America.
- However, ironically on the other hand, there were those proponents of COLORISM who were said to be found mostly among "lighter people", who exhibited social airs which caused them to be perceived by most other "Coloureds" as *"privileged" little princes & princesses"* who, somehow always seemed, (*to their darker brothers & sisters who misunderstood them*), to be loyally-emulating their eminent ruler, that metaphorical **raging "KING"!**
- **But, for the most part, they were NOT really as disloyal as they were perceived to be,...but, *"stuck in the middle"* as they were,...they were simply a very misunderstood group of very good American citizens.**

Nevertheless, as a well-established and sub-cultural segment of America's society,... *"there-they-were",* "the Wesorts", patriotic Americans who were **geographically-separated from both Whites and Blacks**...with their own set of rules, and in their very own private and isolated, clannish little enclaves, comfortably located between two large bodies of water; the Potomac River and the Port Tobacco River, not too far off from the James River; all of them tributaries into the huge & majestic Chesapeake Bay.

"There-they-were", the *BUTLER, GRAY, HARLEY, NEWMAN, PROCTOR, QUEEN, SAVOY, SWANN, and THOMPSON families; which were the core* Wesort families living quietly & peacefully among themselves in the quiet & picturesque little adjacent villages of Port Tobacco & La Plata, in southeast Maryland,...an enclave located far away from the unpredictable chaos & disorganization of the Black communities, while also simultaneously tucked safely away from the cold, prying eyes of the sometimes, very cruel Whites;.. **trying hard to adjust to society's racial laws as best they could,... as an isolated tri-racial Indian, white, & black, = "mixed" and**

very "miX-understood" group of people who were literally caught in the middle of the color- war in America.

So,...as an *isolated* tri-racial group with their very own rigid rules for acceptable moral behavior, racial-etiquette, and ideals,... there they were, closely-resembling another southern ethnic group which ran parallel and contemporaneous to theirs; **the more, better-known, French- speaking "gens-de-couleur libres",** = the "Creoles of Color of New Orleans, Louisiana", who were also **"free-people-of-color".**

Preface

This is the genealogical lineage of the <u>"Proctor-Cook" Family who were</u> one of the "Wesort- Mulatto-Indian" families of Port Tobacco & La Plata, Maryland.
   <u>"The PROCTORS"</u>

<u>Raw Data</u>

<u>(See letters A to- K):</u>

A

The lineage on the attached **genealogical & relationship chart**, shows **direct bloodline-consanguinity** between **#1) Agatha Proctor King, the chief informant of this data,...**
#2) Carmenlita Uter Cook, the genealogical-researcher-author, ... **and #3) Chief Billy "Red Wing" Tayac, the present Chief of Maryland's state-recognized tribe, the Piscataway Indian Nation.**

B

History tells us that as a part of the close-knit "free-people-of-color", Mulatto-Indian ("Wesorts") community of Port Tobacco, & La Plata, in southeast Maryland,...two brothers, **Peter Proctor and William-Noble Proctor, were born circa 1830 & 1831, respectively, in Charles County, Maryland.**

C

As adults, the two brothers became fathers, **with Peter becoming the father of son, William E. Proctor, born circa 1855,........... while around that same time, William-Noble became the father of son, Louis Proctor, also born circa 1855 +/- a few years.**

D

Since their fathers were brothers,... <u>William E. Proctor</u> and <u>Louis Proctor</u> were "first-cousins".

E

In later years, Louis Proctor became father of Philip Sheridan Proctor, born 1895, ...and then many years later, Philip Sheridan Proctor became the father of the present-day Piscataway Indian Chief, Billy "Red Wing" Tayac, born +/- a few years, circa 1936.

F

Please see attached, the eleven (11) "certified" baptismal records from <u>St. Ignatius Catholic Church; a church founded by Father Andrew White, a Jesuit priest, who, in keeping with the Jesuit mission, set out to convert all of Maryland's Native American Indians to Catholicism.</u>

G

<u>This book is the result of extensive research of my father's maternal, Proctor-family of Port Tobacco and adjacent town of La Plata, in southeast, Maryland wherein Agatha Proctor is actually "first-cousin" to my father, Charles Wm. Cook, ...and she is therefore, really my "first-cousin-once-removed".</u>

However, in accordance with the customary procedures followed by fellow genealogists, and the appropriate terminology being utilized by those who practice this profession which dictates that..." your parent's first-cousin is to be called your "aunt- or-uncle", and you are to be called his/her "niece-or-nephew",... **...throughout this book, I will**

henceforth use the term "Aunt Aggie" to describe Agatha Proctor King whenever I may find it necessary to describe something within the context of our familial relationship.

H

The "common progenitors" of Agatha Proctor King and Carmenlita Uter Cook, were William E. Proctor and Mariah Adams, (aka Maria Adams).

With that being said,...let it be known that everything written herein is based on detailed information as it was told to me without alteration, by my wonderful, generous "Aunt", Agatha Proctor King, who this one of the living-daughters of Charles Henry Proctor, the 10 child of William E. Proctor and Maria(h) (Adams) Proctor; (see #10, listed below).

I

William E. Proctor, himself was baptized as an infant at St. Ignatius Church; the Catholic church which was founded by Jesuit priest, Fr. Andrew White for Native Americans' conversion to the Catholic faith.

William E. Proctor became the twice-married father of the following thirteen children, whom were all born, and also all baptized at St. Ignatius Catholic Church, Port Tobacco, Maryland.

William Proctor and Maria(h) Adams were married at St. Ignatius Catholic Church on December 20, 1887. (In addition to William's baptismal record,...please see a certified copy of the marriage certificate, attached, and all the baptismal records of William's children with his first wife, Maria(h) Adams, whom were;

1) Mary-Magdalene "Mamie" Proctor, (child of William, born to Sarah E. Thompson), on 4/10/1884 and baptized 6/01/1884. **2) Sarah Proctor, born 7/15/1889 and baptized 7/21/1889, was grandmother to the author, Carmenlita Uter Cook, aka="Miss Utera".** 3) William Joseph Proctor, born 8/27/1891, and baptized on11/22/1891. 4) Mary Edeny (Edna) Proctor, born 10/10/1892, and baptized on 10/10/1892. 5) Johanna Proctor, born 5/16/1894, and baptized on 5/16/1894. 6) Peter Edward Proctor, born 9/22/1896, and baptized on 9/22/1896.

7) John Quincy Proctor, born 01/10/1901 and baptized on 9/15/1901. 8) Twin to #7, Beale Proctor (= deceased-soon-after-birth). 9) George Proctor, born 8/11/1898 and baptized on 10/25/1898.

J

****Note: **Agatha Proctor King's father, was (#10) Charles Henry Proctor, born 3/01/1902, and baptized on 8/17/1902.**

Note:

(William's first wife, Maria(h) Adams Proctor, died in 1909 when Charles-Henry was only age-7.)

K

William Proctor married a second wife, Mary (Hurd) Beuter to whom were born the following three children.
11) Louis Proctor, = the records are not yet found for Louis' birth or baptismal.
12) Annie Elsie Proctor, born 4/01/1914, and baptized 6/18/1914. 13) **Joseph Lee Proctor, born 4/01/1916, and baptized 5/27/1916.**

Note:
D) William E. Proctor died on November 22, 1918, and was buried at St. Ignatius Catholic Church, Port Tobacco-Maryland on November 24, 1918.
Here, attached are 15 certificates; = the (1)-Certificate of Marriage between William and Maria(h), the (13) Certificates of Baptism, and the (1)-Burial Certificate of William Proctor.

Baptismal Record

Peter Proctor, Jr.

(= born in 1850s).
(the child of Peter Proctor, Senior,... & his wife, Sara Shade),
= (Who is also the brother to William E. Proctor, #2, next.)

Baptismal

William E. Proctor

(= also born in 1850s)
(2nd child of Peter Proctor, "Senior" & his wife, Sara
Shade),...& who is also the BROTHER to #1, above.)

"MISS UTERA"

Marriage Certificate

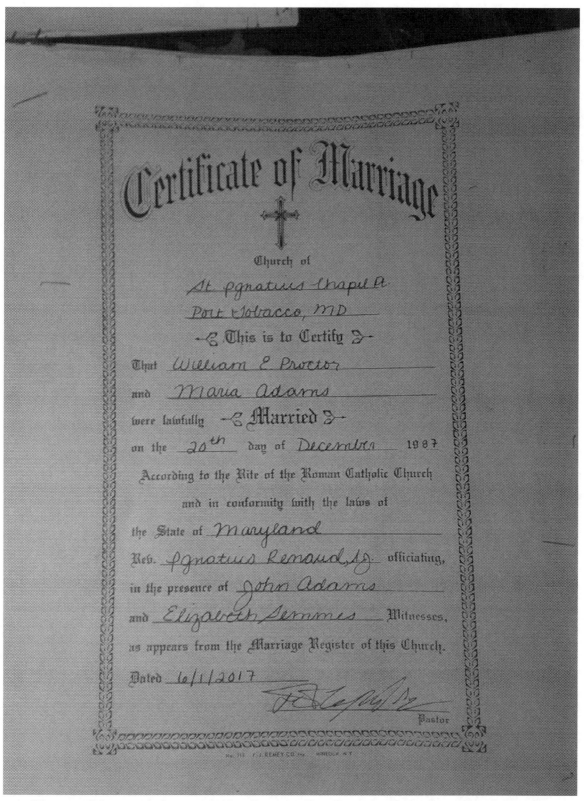

Certificate of Marriage

Church of

St Ignatius Chapel A
Port Tobacco, MD

~ This is to Certify ~

That *William E Proctor*

and *Maria Adams*

were lawfully ~ Married ~

on the *20th* day of *December* 1987

According to the Rite of the Roman Catholic Church

and in conformity with the laws of

the State of *Maryland*

Rev. *Ignatius Renaud, SJ* officiating,

in the presence of *John Adams*

and *Elizabeth Semmes* Witnesses,

as appears from the Marriage Register of this Church.

Dated *6/1/2017*

Pastor

Baptismal

Mary Magdalene Proctor

(Agatha's "Aunt-Mamie")

SARAH PROCTOR

Baptismal

<u>Sarah Proctor</u>

<u>Note:</u> (This is <u>grandmother</u> of the author,
<u>Carmenlita Uter Cook</u>, aka *"Miss Utera"*).

"MISS UTERA"

Baptismal

William Joseph Proctor

Certificate of Baptism

St. Ignatius Church
8855 CHAPEL POINT ROAD
PORT TOBACCO, MD 20677

— This is to Certify —

That _William J. Proctor_

Child of _William Proctor_

and _Mary Adams_

born in _La Plata_ (CITY) _MD_ (STATE)

on the _27th_ day of _August_ 18 91

was

Baptized

on the _22nd_ day of _November_ 19 91

According to the Rite of the Roman Catholic Church

by the Rev. _P.J. O'Connell, S.J._

the Sponsors being _Jennie Mason_

as appears from the Baptismal Register of this Church.

Dated _6/1/17_

_____
Pastor

Baptismal

Mary Edney (Edna) Proctor

Certificate of Baptism

✝

St. Ignatius Church
8855 CHAPEL POINT ROAD
PORT TOBACCO, MD. 20677

— This is to Certify —

That *Mary Edney Proctor*

Child of *William Proctor*

and *Maria Adams*

born in *St. Thomas* (CITY) *MD* (STATE)

on the *10th* day of *October* 18 *92*

was **Baptized**

on the *10th* day of *October* 18 *92*

According to the Rite of the Roman Catholic Church

by the Rev. *James Gardiner, S.J.*

the Sponsors being { *Susan Jenifer*

as appears from the Baptismal Register of this Church.

Dated *6/1/17*

[signature] Pastor

No. 314 F. J. REMEY CO., INC. MINEOLA, N.Y.

Baptismal

Johanna Proctor

Certificate of Baptism

St. Ignatius Church
8855 CHAPEL POINT ROAD
PORT TOBACCO, MD 20677

~ This is to Certify ~

That _Johanna Proctor_

Child of _William Proctor_

and _Maria Adams_

born in _Port Tobacco_ (CITY) _MD_ (STATE)

on the _16th_ day of _May_ 18 _94_

was **Baptized**

on the _16th_ day of _May_ 18 _94_

According to the Rite of the Roman Catholic Church

by the Rev. _James Gardiner, S.J._

the Sponsors being _Elizabeth Simmes_

as appears from the Baptismal Register of this Church.

Dated _6/6/17_

_____ Pastor

WESORT-MULATTO-INDIANS (AN ETHNIC TRI-RACIAL ISOLATE GROUP) OF PORT TOBACCO AND LA PLATA, MARYLAND

Baptismal

Peter Edward Proctor

Certificate of Baptism

St. Ignatius Church
8855 CHAPEL POINT ROAD
PORT TOBACCO, MD 20677

~ This is to Certify ~

That *Peter Edward Proctor*
Child of *William E Proctor*
and *Maria Adams*
born in *La Plata* (CITY) *MD* (STATE)
on the *22nd* day of *september* 18 *96*
was

Baptized

on the *22nd* day of *September* 18 *96*
According to the Rite of the Roman Catholic Church
by the Rev. *John J. Rodock, S.J.*
the Sponsors being { *Molly Simms*

as appears from the Baptismal Register of this Church.

Dated *6/1/17*

Pastor

Baptismal

John Quincy Proctor

Certificate of Baptism

St. Ignatius Church
8655 CHAPEL POINT ROAD
PORT TOBACCO, MD 20677

This is to Certify

That _John Quincy Proctor_
Child of _William Proctor_
and _Maria Adams_
born in _La Plata_ (CITY) _MD_ (STATE)
on the _10th_ day of _January_ 19 _01_
was
Baptized
on the _15th_ day of _September_ 19 _01_
According to the Rite of the Roman Catholic Church
by the Rev. _John B Meuser, S.J._
the Sponsors being { _Nana Royer_

as appears from the Baptismal Register of this Church.

Dated _6/1/17_

_____
Pastor

No Baptismal Record exists for

Twin, Beale Proctor because

(This twin to John Quincy, died at birth)

Baptismal

George Proctor

Certificate of Baptism

St. Ignatius Church
8855 CHAPEL POINT ROAD
PORT TOBACCO, MD 20677

— This is to Certify —

That *George Proctor*

Child of *William Proctor*

and *Maria Adams*

born in *La Plata* (CITY) *MD* (STATE)

on the *11th* day of *August* 1898

was

Baptized

on the *25th* day of *October* 1898

According to the Rite of the Roman Catholic Church

by the Rev. *John P. M. Schleuter, S.J.*

the Sponsors being { *Elizabeth Sims*

as appears from the Baptismal Register of this Church.

Dated *6/1/17*

Pastor

Baptismal

<u>Charles Henry Proctor</u>

<u>Note:</u> (This is father of <u>Agatha Proctor King</u>, the <u>family-tree/research</u> informant.)

Louis Proctor

No Baptismal Record has been found yet for

this child, = <u>the first-born child</u> of

William E. Proctor

with

his 2nd wife, Mary Hurd Beuter

****

Baptismal Record

Annie Elsie Proctor

Baptismal

Joseph Lee Proctor

Certificate of Baptism

St. Ignatius Church
8855 CHAPEL POINT ROAD
PORT TOBACCO, MD 20677

— This is to Certify —

That _Joseph Lee Proctor_

Child of _William Proctor_

and _Mary Beutel_

born in _La Plata_ (CITY) _MD_ (STATE)

on the _1st_ day of _April_ 19 _16_

was **Baptized**

on the _27th_ day of _May_ 19 _16_

According to the Rite of the Roman Catholic Church

by the Rev. _C.H. Bridges, S.J._

the Sponsors being _Julia Johnson_

as appears from the Baptismal Register of this Church.

Dated _6/14/17_

_____
Pastor

Death Certificate

William E. Proctor

St. Ignatius-Chapel Point
8855 Chapel Point Road
Port Tobacco, MD 20677

Notice of Funeral and Interment

This notice confirms that

William Proctor

then residing in Washington, DC

died on November 22, 1918

and

was buried at St. Ignatius-Chapel Point

on November 24, 1918.

Proof of Piscataway Indian ancestry:

Following the certified documents, attached hereto, is a "relationship chart" which shows the connection between <u>my paternal grandmother, Sarah Proctor, (child, #2), (and also her sibling, <u>Charles Henry Proctor (child #10), - Agatha's father,...</u> showing BOTH as <u>being "first-cousins" to Philip Sheridan Proctor</u>, thereby making my aunt, <u>Agatha Proctor</u> and <u>I, Carmenlita Uter Cook, "first-cousin, (1X) once-removed"</u>, and <u>"first-cousin-(2X) twice-removed"</u>, respectively to the present-day chief of the Piscataway Indian Nation; <u>Chief Billy "Redwing" Tayac.</u>

Needless to say, the Proctor-Cook family-tree has grown exponentially to incredibly, enormous proportions, and to undertake research of it would be a great challenge for even the most extraordinaire and world-renowned genealogist (which I certainly do not claim to be!)

After taking that overwhelming and mind-boggling challenge into consideration, I decided to "back-up", and limit my research to two direct lines, which are #1, the <u>PROCTOR-Y-DNA</u> of my great-grandfather, William E. Proctor, (Sarah's father), and #2, the <u>COOK-Y-DNA</u> direct line of my own father, the late, Charles William Cook, a successful businessman, and founder of the East Side Cab Company, which in the 1940s & 1950s was located in Washington, DC.

Therefore, the ultimate goal of this research was to show that we, the "Proctor-Cooks", are related by blood to the chief of the present "Piscataway Indian Nation", Billy "Redwing" Tayac.

In order to do so, it was necessary for me, firstly, to find and research a person with specific male-DNA, which goes directly back to William E. Proctor, our common progenitor.

Thankfully, <u>I found such a willing participant in Paul Michael Proctor, the son of Charles Henry Proctor, who is also the "full-sibling" and brother to Agatha Proctor King.</u>

<u>IMPORTANT!</u>

<u>(A male-dna volunteer is STILL NEEDED for
the ROBERT COOK male dna-line!)</u>
<u>If YOU, the reader, are that person, please call 929-404-3205!</u>
<u>Thank you!</u>

For the Proctor research I had successfully located <u>Paul Michael Proctor</u>,… so, at Agatha's home on Easter-Sunday, (<u>April 16, 2017</u>), I gathered the dna- samples, by way of buccal swabs, of four people; = Agatha, Aggie's brother, <u>Paul</u>,…her daughter, Linnette, and her grand-son, <u>Charles-"Chucky"</u>.

Then, those samples were immediately sent, thereafter, to the FTDNA research laboratory in Houston, Texas, and <u>after waiting about eight weeks, the research-results came back, and they successfully showed that Paul's male, Y-DNA goes back to "NATIVE AMERICAN – United States"</u>.

Photos of <u>Chief Billy Tayac</u>, leader of the <u>Piscataway Indian Nation</u>, anointing the author's family with the <u>sacred "eagle feather"</u>, to show recognition of the family as belonging to the <u>Piscataway Indians</u>.

<u>One of the greatest honors among all Native American tribes, is to be given recognition as belonging to the native American people with anointment by an Indian chief with the sacred eagle feather.</u>

<u>Below, please see, Carmenlita-Uter-Cook, her son, Michael-Lehmann, and her grand-daughter, Sharmaine-Lehmann-Pierre (age-8) receiving anointment by the chief, Billy "Red Wing Tayac.</u>

<u>*These photos were taken at an 'Awakening of the Earth' ceremony at Mayaone Reserve, Accokeek, Maryland (in April, 2008).</u>

Page
36-A

It is important <u>to note here</u> that Paul's Y-DNA also belongs to his sister, Agatha Proctor King, as it was also clearly indicated in the DNA-results that Paul & Agatha are "full siblings'.

Special Notice

Through the y-dna testing of Paul Proctor (brother of Agatha Proctor, (aka "Aggie-King"), the FTDNA-test-results clearly states that the "PROCTOR-branch" of the "Proctor-Cook" blood-lines go directly back to the "Native Americans of the United States of America".

Thus, the following chart on this "relationship page" proves our direct lineage back to Native Americans,... however it is not presently exhibited here because this information will NOT be open to the general public at this time, but instead, will be accessible and privy ONLY to those family-members, whom "upon special request & participation", actively donate the needed "ancestral photographs" as are described on page 33* of this book,.....<u>and with the full agreement & clear understanding that those "requested photos" must be submitted to the author/ publisher, "Miss Utera", with a signed release, to permit the photos to be used by this author, to publish Part 2, as an updated copy of this same book.</u>

<u>Edition #2)</u> which will be solely about the <u>COOK-branch of this family lineage, using the male, Y-dna test-results of the direct descendants of our progenitor, Robert Cook,</u> = who was the <u>husband of</u> Sarah Proctor Cook, and <u>father of</u> Charles Wm. Cook, <u>to whom this book is partially-dedicated.</u>

The names of the <u>Cook Sisters</u>, under their photo <u>will be released when permission is sent by next-of-kin, to the author by TEXT message only, @ 929-404-3205.</u>

<u>Please send photos of parents of Robert Cook, Robert Cook, Sarah Proctor, William E. Proctor, Mariah-Adams-Proctor.</u>

<u>Also needed are photos of (1) William "Billy Cook, = who was the first son of Charles Wm.Cook, "Senior" and an unknown-mother;... and "Junior", whose full name is Charles Cook, "JUNIOR", son of Lillian Cook & Charles Cook, "SENIOR".</u>

Family-tree / Relationship Chart

The information on this chart is private, and will be released to the **SMITHSONIAN Institute**…the **Maryland Genealogical Society,** and to certain family-members, **upon their donation of the needed photographs requested on previous pages of this book.)**

Cousin Chart

How are we related to each other?

Follow the instructions, and the "cousin chart" below, will easily explain how to identify your relationships to your relatives.

1) See the numbers from 0 to 6 across the top and down the side of the chart.
2) Each number indicates the number of generations "removed" = away, from a common ancestor.
3) "CA" in the the upper left square represents the "common ancestor".
4) Figure out WHO is the ancestor that you share with another person.
5) For example, use you mother as the "CA", then place one finger on number 1 at the TOP of the chart.
6) Notice that the letter immediately under #1 is S which means son (or daughter), and it shows that a son is only one generation from the "CA" = common ancestor.
7) Then place one finger on number 2 at the TOP of the chart, and you see now that the letters immediately under the #2 are GS , and it means "grandson" (or granddaughter), and you can also see that a grandson (or granddaughter) is two (2) generations "removed" (= away) from the "CA" = common ancestor.
8) Now place your finger on #1 at the SIDE of the chart, and also on # 1 at the TOP.
9) Bring the side-finger over horizontally until it is under the same column as the one (#1) at the TOP of the chart.
10) Bring the two fingers together until they meet, and you will see the letter V in the square, which means "brother" (or sister). That means the "CA" is the mother of both, the person represented by the SIDE # and also the person represented by the TOP #.
11) Now place the TOP finger on #2, and also the SIDE finger on #2. Bring the two fingers together until they meet at the square that has 1C in the square 1C means "1ˢᵗ cousin", and shows also that both of the #2s are two generations "removed" from the "CA" who is their grandmother.
12) Now place a finger on #1/TOP and on #2/SIDE. Bring the two fingers together until they meet in the square marked N. N means that one of the persons, either SIDE or TOP is a niece (or nephew) to the other person, indicating that one person is an uncle (or aunt) with the same "CA" = common ancestor.
13) 1C1R means "first cousin, once removed" = you are my first cousin, one generation away.
14) The chart continues with the same pattern throughout.
15) Study the chart by using the name of a family-member on the SIDE, and a different family-member on the TOP. Draw the fingers together to find out the relationship.

	0	1	2	3	4	5	6
0	CA	S	GS	GGS	GGS	GGS	GGS
1	S	V	N	GN	GGN	2 GGN	3 GGN
2	GS	N	1C	1C 1R	1C 2R	1C 3R	1C 4R
3	GGS	GN	1C 1R	2C	2C 1R	2C 2R	2C 3R
4	2 GGS	GGN	1C 2R	2C 1R	3C	3C 1R	3C 2R
5	3 GGS	GGN	1C 3R	2C 2R	3C 1R	4C	4C 1R
6	4 GGS	3 GGN	1C 4R	2C 3R	3C 2R	4C 1R	5C

CA   Common Ancestor
C   Cousin
V   Brother or sister
R   Times removed
S   Son or daughter
N   Nephew or niece
GS   Grandson or granddaughter
GGS Great-grandson or great-granddaughter

1924 Baker Roll Search Form

To be enrolled as a member of the Eastern Band of the Cherokee Indians you must have a direct lineal ancestor on the 1924 Baker Roll. This form is **NOT** an application for membership. Fill out this form with the names of your ancestors and the Tribal Enrollment office will search the 1924 Baker Roll to determine if your ancestors appear. Please return this completed form to:

Tribal Enrollment Office
PO Box 2069
Cherokee, NC 28719

Your Information

Your Name: Carmelita "Carmen" Cook *Carmelita*		Date of Birth:
Mailing address: P.O. Box 1268 @ Cooper Station		City: New York
State: New York	Zip Code: 10276 County: Manhattan	Telephone #:

Your Biological Parents Information (Only list your Cherokee ancestors.)

Name of Father (Paternal): Charles Wm. Cook		Date of Birth: 12/12/1910
Place of Birth: Washington, D.C.	Date of Death: 5/22/1956	Place of Death: Washington, D.C.
Name of Mother (Maternal): Helena Utera		Date of Birth: 8/03/1919
Place of Birth: Sea Islands, SC	Date of Death: January 5, 2000	Place of Death: New York City

Your Ancestors Information. (Circle Maternal or Paternal. Only list Cherokee ancestors.)

Name of Paternal / Maternal Grandfather: Robert Cook		Date of Birth: March 16, 1890
Place of Birth: Spartanburg, S.C.	Date of Death: November, 1948	Place of Death: Washington, D.C.
Name of Paternal / (Maternal) Grandmother: Sarah Proctor		Date of Birth: 7/15/1889
Place of Birth: La Plata, Maryland	Date of Death: May, 1922	Place of Death: Washington, D.C.
Name of (Paternal) / Maternal G-Grandfather: William E. Proctor		Date of Birth: circa 1855
Place of Birth: Port Tobacco, Maryland	Date of Death: November 23, 1918	Place of Death: Washington, D.C.
Name of Paternal / (Maternal) GG-Grandmother: Maria(h) Adams		Date of Birth: circa 1860
Place of Birth: Port Tobacco, Maryland	Date of Death: 1929	Place of Death: Washington, D.C.
Name of (Paternal) / Maternal GG-Grandfather: Peter Proctor	Date of Death:	Date of Birth: circa 1830
Place of Birth: Port Tobacco, Maryland	Date of Death:	Place of Death: Maryland
Name of Paternal / (Maternal) GG-Grandmother: Sarah Shale		Date of Birth: circa 1831
Place of Birth: Port Tobacco, Md.	Date of Death:	Place of Death: Maryland
Name of Paternal / Maternal GGG-Grandfather: William Proctor		Date of Birth: circa 1790
Place of Birth: Port Tobacco, Md.	Date of Death:	Place of Death: Maryland
Name of Paternal / Maternal GGG-Grandmother:		Date of Birth:
Place of Birth:	Date of Death:	Place of Death:

If you have any additional ancestors you would like have searched for on the 1924 Baker Roll please list them below: Remember direct lineal ancestry only. (Aunts, uncles, and cousins are not direct lineal ancestors.)

Name: Mingle Elmore	Date of Birth:	Date of Death:
Name: Armstrong Elmore	Date of Birth:	Date of Death:
Name:	Date of Birth:	Date of Death:
Name:	Date of Birth:	Date of Death:
Name:	Date of Birth:	Date of Death:

Revised!
Tab (2)
Attachments/ Cherokee Nation Card # 573 54907 (2) Retired - Baker Roll # 910

Please send only the information requested above. While pictures and family history statements are fascinating and of much value to your individual family, they do not have any bearing in searching the 1924 Baker Roll and they may be damaged during the mailing process.

"MISS UTERA"

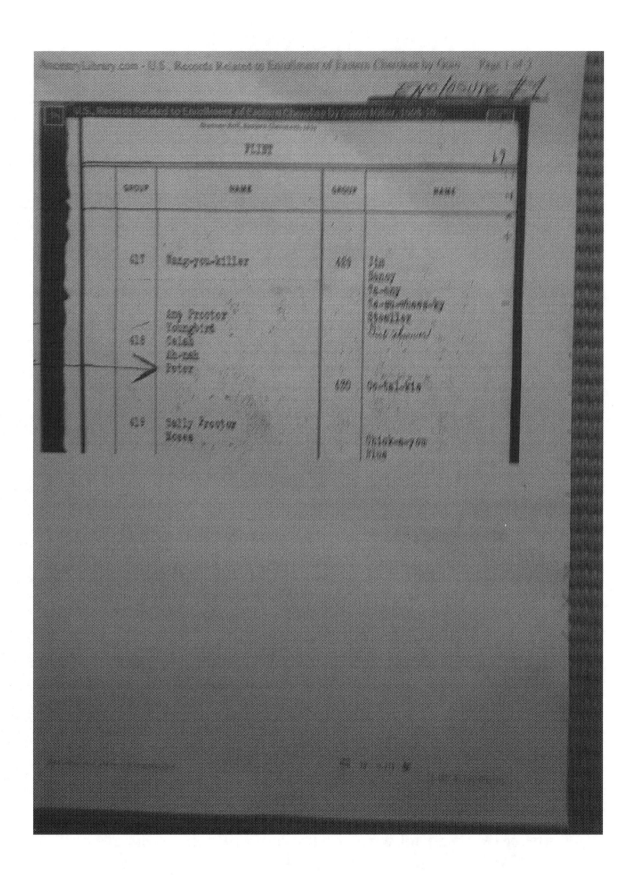

**PHOTO OF AUTHOR WITH HER TWO (2) GRANDDAUGHTERS
STANDING IN FRONT OF WENDY'S.**

**PHOTOGRAPH OF AUTHOR WITH TWO (2) GRAND-DAUGHTERS, SHARMAINE
& MELODY ON HORSEBACK AT THE PISCATAWAY "POW-WOW".**

THREE COUSINS IN FRONT OF ST. IGNATIUS CHURCH, PORT TOBACCO, MARYLAND.

THREE COUSINS; MIKEY, SHA-SHA, & MELLY.

"MISS UTERA"

ST. IGNATIUS
1798

WESORT-MULATTO-INDIANS (AN ETHNIC TRI-RACIAL ISOLATE GROUP) OF PORT
TOBACCO AND LA PLATA, MARYLAND   43

**PHOTOS ON EASTER SUNDAY, 2010, FOLLOWING AN EASTER-EGG HUNT,…
@ ST. IGNATIUS CHURCH; WITH EGGS HIDDEN IN THE-CEMETERY!**

IT WAS <u>FUN</u> FOR THE KIDS!

THE AUTHORS' 3 GRANDCHILDREN, MIKE(AGE-17), MELODY (AGE-7) &
SHARMAINE (AGE-10), STANDING IN FRONT OF **PROCTOR** HEADSTONE.

As a special gift of my appreciation to "Aunt Aggie" for her absolute devotion to this project as I went through the arduous task of genealogical research,... **and for her very dedicated and excellent assistance**, always giving me all her time over the telephone each and every day for the past eleven (16) straight months, while showering me with relentless loyalty as she offered to me, such a wealth of enriched details on the history of the Proctor family,.... A special dna-test was done on Agatha Proctor's MtDNA (mitochondrial line), and the results came back showing that her mother's ancestry of her Gray & Savoy lineages, go back to the countries of East & West-Asia, India, Pakistan, France, Eastern Europe, & Africa, etc. In addition special research is being done on Aggie's SAVOY lineage.

Those very same, aforementioned dna-results are the profound attestation as to WHY there existed before, and still exists today, WITHIN one family; = the Proctor-Cook family, the diversity of so many Native-American-Indian, mulatto and quadroon phenotypes of blonde, brown, and/or black, straight, wavy, curly, and/ or tightly coiled hair, matched with skin-complexions that range the entire color- spectrum, from dark-sepia to fair-white, with dark-brown eyes and also very many with light-colored blue, green, & grey eyes found throughout the entire family tree.

In regard to the MtDNA (mitochondrial) results, it is important to remember that since Agatha and Paul Proctor share the same mother, the MtDNA results apply to Paul, as well as to their other full-siblings.

The Y-DNA results were also deemed highly successful by proving both Agatha and Paul to be descendants of Native Americans. The one thing that was of most importance to me, personally,...is that the dna-results also clearly proved that Agatha Proctor King and Paul Michael Proctor are both my dna-proven, first-cousins-1x-removed, and were therefore proven to have been first-cousins to my father, Charles Wm. Cook, Senior, who was the son of Robert Cook and Sarah Proctor.

After the dna-results came back, my dilemma for full satisfaction, was to prove not only a "paper-trail", but also a dna-match directly to the chief, Billy Tayac, leader of Maryland's state-recognized Indian tribe; the Piscataway Indian Nation.

I already knew that acquiring a dna-match would've been nearly an almost, impossible feat because of the fact that those specific Proctors who are tribal members, tend to be very closed with their genealogical information, and I, of course, understand that, since such exclusivity is for good reasons; = in order to protect the Proctor legacy, from the over-zealous, ambitious interlopers who, due to highly-charged racism and colorism during that era), for many years have wanted to marry into the Proctor family's prominence, merely because ... an extreme amount of importance **was placed on the tri-racial-isolated "Wesort-families" of the pre-civil-rights era, who possessed the** surnames of <u>Butler, Gray, Harley, Newman, Proctor, Queen, Savoy, Swann, and Thompson,</u> and also because so many of the members of the Wesort families then possessed phenotypes of the highly-valued light-skin and/or the very treasured & sought-after, so-called "good-hair".

Genealogical Chart

of the

SAVOY FAMILY

in France

Private Information.

Aunt Aggie's grandmother's maiden name, *(= "Grandma-Penny")* was a SAVOY, as she was the daughter of a French man who had married her Indian mother in Maryland.

****

PHOTO REQUEST!

Requested SAVOY Photo-Donations are REQUIRED for this SAVOY lineage chart which required extensive laborious research

Back then, in the USA, race-mixing was AGAINST-THE-LAW and punishable by time in the federal penitentiary.

So, the colorism trend, back then, *during the post Civil-War era*, which stemmed from white-supremacy, was that everybody wanted to be "light-skinned" as possible and to have as so-called "good-hair" as possible, "like the Proctors had".

Therefore, during that era, when interracial-marriages were practically non-existent and outlawed in most of the United States,... it was a common practice among many southern women,= (especially the darker-toned, Black women of DMV (= D.C., Maryland and Virginia),..., to make it their "goals", "to-marry-a-Proctor- man" just in order to acquire the Proctor surname through marriage, ...or if not "a Proctor man", at least to attain one-of-those other nine (9) previously mentioned core surnames, = (Butler, Gray, Harley, Newman, Proctor, Queen, Savoy, Swann, Thompson), and/or '...to marry Newman-man,...a Savoy-man...or a Swann, etc.,....and,...in addition to that, to acquire the "Wesort-physical-traits-&-phenotypes" for their children.

Yes, back then, t'was definitely all about color while white-supremacy prevailed!

But, ironically, due to those very same over-zealous "goals", the phenotypes have become altered quite a bit in the opposite direction, as although most "Wesorts" are still of a lighter hue, many of the children of the newer generations have become increasingly much darker-skinned as time has gone by.

In fact, I learned that things have changed so much so, that at the Annual "Proctor- Day Picnic" that used to be held in Maryland each year,... the picnic has now been mostly abandoned by the so-called "lighter"-and-"good-haired" Proctors who are no longer abundantly visible as attendees, but nowadays, instead, are more apt to be found at the annual Indian "pow-wows" held all over the USA, as well as at the other Native American celebrations known as "Awakening of-the Earth", "Green Corn" and other feast days, held all over the Americas and Canada every year on the various Indian reservations where they... (the Wesort-descendants)... *nowadays*, mostly identify themselves as Native-American-Piscataway-Indians, not seeming to want to identify with the old-school terminology of "Wesort" anymore.

In fact, many tribal-members now consider usage of the term, "Wesort" to be rather insulting, and INSIST, instead, on being referred to as a "Piscataway Indian".

Are the "Wesorts" now an extinct ethnic group? or, is it true that a rose by another name, is still always a rose?? My question is: Are "Wesorts" now EXTINCT????,.... or merely "roses being called by another name?" I will let YOU decide.

As a genealogical-researcher **without access to ALL the dna-results** that are needed for scientific-proof,...... I find that **many of us must still rely a great deal on the "paper-trails".**

While relying on those "paper trails", I have discovered that the ones that I have had in my possession for many (30+) years, ... do indeed, show me that our family's "Proctor line" leads us directly back to the Piscataway Indian Nation of Maryland.

In addition, it has been rumored that my paternal great-grandmother, Maria(h) Adams Proctor (*William E. Proctor's first wife*) may be descended from the family of <u>President John Quincy Adams.</u> Although I have found that Maria(h)'s father was, indeed, a man named John Adams, who was married to her mother Rachel Semmes,... thus far I have no proof that, the "presidential claim" of "a John Adams" has actually been traced back, specifically the 6th USA-president. My sister, who knows more about this family-legacy from our dear Aunt Faye's having taken "them" to visit an Adams Mansion in Virginia,...will <u>hopefully</u> be the one who takes on this research as her "baby". I, however, at this point, must <u>digress.</u>

Summary

I do know, however, that <u>William E. Proctor and Maria(h) Adams were the progenitors of this branch of our family-tree,</u> and since they were the main focus of my research,... as a member of this lineage, I feel that I have satisfactorily done my due diligence on the Proctor side, by proving that our bloodlines are descended from Maryland and the "Native Americans of the United States of America".

In the future, further research by one or more of the numerous younger-generational-descendants of this family-tree, may one day decide to take on the task of researching more evidence to prove the veracity of the aforementioned, "John Adams-presidential-rumor".

My personal hope is that at least a few of the Wesort-Piscataway people whom are directly descended from the nine (9) core surnames of the DMV (DC, Maryland & Virginia), <u>will indeed engage themselves in genealogical research in order to provide the historians at the Smithsonian Institute with more information, photographs, and family-tree charts of the other tri-racial isolate families,...in addition to copies of their Butler, Gray, Harley, Newman, Proctor, Queen, Savoy, Swann, and Thompson family-trees,...which is what I will be doing by donating this book to the Smithsonian and the Maryland Genealogical Society, for the good of public interest.</u>

Genealogical-Research-Assistance- To-Others-Who-Are-Doing-Research

I regret that I no longer accept research clients,...however, my research back to my paternal great-grandparents, **William E. Proctor** and **Maria(h) Adams Proctor**,... shows results which, **when correctly used**, and **employed as a pattern to follow**, should serve **as a guide to assist other members of this very same Proctor-Cook family-tree**, in order to complete their own future researches, especially anyone who is descended from one of William Proctor's thirteen children, **of whom, I am sure, there are hundreds, and even thousands more of their descendants;**....and/or **from the Y-DNA lineage of Robert Cook who was Sarah Proctor's husband, and my paternal grand-father.**

Important Request

Nowadays, I function primarily as an "archivist" (records-keeper), who no longer engages in "paper-trail" genealogical research, per se, = **NOT for any amount of money whatsoever! = por absolutamente NADA! = Too much work for me, nowadays.!!!!!**

However, in the very last analysis of this particular **PROCTOR-COOK project**,... in order to complete research of my father's lineage, **I am hereby EMPHATICALLY requesting that at least two willing male-participants of different mothers,...who have within their bodies, the male, Y-dna which traces directly back to Robert Cook,... to PLEASE COME FORTH and agree to make an offer to submit their dna in the form of buccal swabs, to my affiliated, online genealogical company, FTDNA.**

• •

Please!
go online to:
FTDNA, @Wesorts-Piscataway.com.

Compensation

All **appropriate male, Y-DNA** offers to participate will be greatly appreciated and monetarily-compensated, **if demanded!**

Males who wish to participate, and who descend directly <u>along the male-line</u> <u>from Robert Cook, should go online to the website and apply to become a member</u> <u>of the Wesorts-Piscataway, dual-geographical, group project at FTDNA.com,</u> <u>(Family Tree DNA).</u>

Other descendants of the nine (9) core surnames<u>, (= Butler, Gray, Harley, Newman,</u> <u>Proctor, Queen, Savoy, Swann, & Thompson),</u> interested in becoming members of the on-going, **<u>MULINDIAN NATION research-project, which is about the</u>** **"<u>Mulattos of Maryland</u>"** called "**Wesorts**", and also about other mixed-Indians of Virginia, and Delaware should **go on <u>GOOGLE</u>** to:

<u>FTDNA, Wesort-Piscataways.com.</u>

NEW PROJECT

Melungeons as "ship-wrecked Portuguese:

The "<u>Wesorts</u>" <u>ethnic group</u> was/is one of the smaller tri-racial groups which is derived from, and evolved out of, the much larger and more well-known group of "tri-racial-isolates" known as the "<u>Melungeons</u>" by renowned anthropologists and historians.

It has been verified <u>time & again</u> that <u>the Melungeons</u> are the **descendants of Portuguese seamen who were forced to disembark from a ship-wrecked vessel in the early 1800s or late 1700s somewhere on or close to Chesapeake Bay near Virginia, Maryland and the Carolinas.**

Many people coming from the "Melungeons", have theorized that the term has an etymological derivation from the middle-east.

But I, strongly feels that the term may derive from a southern accented corruption of "Mulatto-Injuns" that makes it sound like "Melungeons".

In addition to being called <u>"Mulatto-Injuns"</u>, (among several other appellations), we Wesorts were also called <u>"Chesapeake-Creoles"</u>...(which must NOT be confused with the "Louisiana-French-Creoles"... or the "Massachusetts & Rhode Island- (CapeVerdean) Portuguese-Crioulos").

Although we have a very, slightly different history from the "French-Creoles of Louisiana", and the "Portuguese-Creoles" of the New England states of Massachusetts and Rhode Island,.....basically-speaking we "Chesapeake-Creoles" are the same type of "triracial-European/Indian/African mixed-race-people" who were brought to the mainland USA in the Americas, whilst speaking either English, French, German, Spanish or Portuguese, the languages of our colonizers from England, France, Germany/Dutch-Netherlands, Spain or Portugal,... and our surnames sometimes reflect those ancestries; for example Savoy is French, and Proctor is British.

Many of us "Creoles" have lost our "original languages skills", while many others in places like Martinique, Aruba, Hispaniola, etc., ...have successfully maintained them.

On the inside FRONT-COVER, available to see, is a map of the various groups known to historians as "tri-racial isolated groups"; and on that map "Wesorts" is shown with an arrow pointing directly to our area of Maryland, located on the Chesapeake Bay.

<u>As I bring to closure, the research of my father's lineage back to the Native Americans,...I hereby announce that I now have another, entirely NEW PROJECT, which is focused on our "mixed" languages, the "creole-lingua-francas".</u>

If what the historians say, *(and what I, myself believe)*, is factual, = (that the Melingeon-Wesorts" are Portuguese-descent),...and that the Wesorts in fact, derived from the **Portuguese-Melungeons)...**then I, *Carmenlita Uter Cook,.........the author of this book, aka "Miss Utera",...* am of "**double-Portuguese**" ancestry, which I inherited through <u>both</u> my father's "**Chesapeake-Creole/Wesorts**" lineage,... and also my mother's lineage via my maternal grand-father's bloodlines back to the **HURTERE (=HUTRA/UTRA-HUTER/UTER/UTERA,& DUTRA)**

families of Fayal-island-Azores- Portugal who migrated in the late 1700s/early 1800s, **to La Ceiba-Honduras,… British Honduras,… then New Orleans -Louisiana, and Charleston, South-Carolina.**

My maternal grand-father, who was a merchant seaman, was born in Belize City, British Honduras (= which is now an independent country called BELIZE

So,…moving on, my main linguistics/genealogical-focus will now be <u>to trace back to the specific boat that in the 1800s, had brought my mother's Huter/ Uter/Utera family over from Fayal- Azores-Portugal to Central America, (= into Honduras & Belize).</u>

<u>I think such a journey will be fun, and I am looking forward to it!</u>

LINGUISTICS

Since I am **"double-(2X)-Portuguese"**, descended from both the **Melungeons** of my father's **Wesort people**, and the **Azorean-Portuguese of my mother's father,...** under the auspices of the **Creole-American/Amerindian Genealogical Society, Inc., founded in 1983)...** the main goal of my "new project" will be to show how the vernacular of Portugal had linguistic influences upon Melungeons,... Azorean-families,... Cape Verdean families,...Brazilian families,...and the families of Portuguese-speaking-Angola-Africa.

The goal is to analyze and to bring to the general public, the information of a creolized–cultural historical-past which is not usually taught in the schools of the USA.

The goal will be to demonstrate the linguistic connections between genealogy (family-trees), the Creole (Crioulo) languages spoken by those families, and its effect upon its biracial/ tri-racial history.

The people, like myself, whom have always identified ourselves as "Creoles", have historically always maintained within our minds, **"a mentally-distinct culture"** which sets us apart from mainstream society as **"not-white", but "not black, either.**

"Our people" have always been "UNDER-THE-RADAR, mixed-race, "COLOUREDs", (= whom are also NOT Black & NOT White"),...but the light-skinned, & copper- toned, curly-haired, coily, & not kinky,...but, good-graded-**"krinkly-"haired people of the USA-of-America"** whom were derived from the traditional tri-racial "mixtures" that evolved out of American **colonization & slavery** (which always go hand in hand).

We are the people whom are <u>derived from</u> and originate out of the "tri-racial, bi-racial isolated groups" shown on the map of Tri-Racial Indian Groups shown on the map at the first two pages of this book.), ...isolated people, who throughout the history of the USA, have been very **carefully-scrutinized by historians and anthropologists, and other intellectuals whom have testified that "WE" have shown among ourselves, to have behavioral characteristics which are quite different from that of other Americans;...characteristics which can be witnessed among the traditional mannerisms & moral tenets of not all, but of most of the Massachusetts-Azorean & Cape Verdean-Portuguese-Crioulos,... the Belizean-Creoles,...the Louisiana-French-Creoles,... the Virginia-Washington-DC/Maryland-Wesorts,...**

Louisiana-Redbones,... the West-Virginia-Guineas,... the Virginia-Pamunkey & Mattaponi,... the Long Island-Shinnecocks,... the Connecticut-Mashantucket-Pequots,... the Rhode Island Narragansetts,... the North Carolina Lumbees,... and the South Carolina Turks & Brass-Ankles, etc.

Most of us know who we are, **most of the time!**

Creole Languages

The languages of "our people", the tri-racial people, are the "creole-lingua-francas" which evolved out of the American slavery/colonization-eras are:

1) UK=England = British English and South Carolina/Georgia Sea Island (**"Geechee/Gullah-patwa-creole"**), Barbados (**"Bajan"**), **"Belizean-Creole"**, or Jamaican (**"Patois"**). 2) Portugal = Portuguese & (**"Crioulo"**) as is spoken in Azores, Angola, Brazil, CapeVerde, Mozambique and Massachuetts. 3) France = French & "**Haitian-Creole** [Kreyol]" and **"Louisiana-Creole"**. 4) German (= **"Old-Dutch"**) = (**"Papiamentu"**) as is spoken in Aruba, Bonaire, & Curacao.
5) Spanish as is spoken in Puerto Rico, Belize, Bolivia, Cuba, Dominican Republic, Guatemala & Honduras.

As the languages were being "mixed" and became "creole-languages",….our bloodlines were simultaneously being "mixed to make us the "Creole-people" who we are today.

SCHOLARSHIPS

<u>"Lost-Creole-Language"</u> scholarship-requirements are presently being established.

You may prove that <u>you qualify for this scholarship</u> if:

(A)…you are a "mixed-race', <u>mulatto or biracial person</u> who is a descendant of one of the "creole-language-groups" of the "conquistadores/ =European "colonizers".

(B) …due to slavery and/or emigration to the Americas, you have "lost" use of the family's original creole-lingua-franca.

(C)...you have serious interest in seriously undertaking **ADVANCED STUDY** of **both** the old-world **European language and its affiliated creole-lingua-franca (idiom).**

(D) ...**you can prove** by your own genealogical **"language-trail" and scientific dna-research that you are directly descended from two persons who participated in the colonial, marriage-system known as "placage".**

Edition 2

****

The "COOKS"

The publication of this edition <u>is contingent upon sufficient photo-donations.</u> <u>If ever published, this edition of the book will contain:</u>

8) A long list of <u>("late 1800s & early (1900s)-marriages")</u> of all the people formerly known as ethnic group called "Wesort-Indians" in southern Maryland, but whom are now called "Piscataway Indians".

9) Cousin chart. 10) Consanguinity chart (Marriage Laws = marriage approval-relationship-chart of the Catholic Church). 11) Family-tree chart – 5 generations, (blank). 12) Family-tree chart – 9 generations, (blank). 13) St. Ignatius Catholic Church @ Port Tobacco, Maryland.

PHOTOGRAPH OF AUTHOR, WITH HER FATHER, <u>CHARLES WM. COOK</u>, AND BROTHER, REGGIE.

PHOTO OF THE FIVE (5) DAUGHTERS OF AUTHOR'S FATHER, CHARLES WM. COOK.

J.,…E.,…C.,…C.,…AND D.

(NAMES WILL BE RELEASED IN EDITION #2, WHEN PERMISSION IS GRANTED BY NEAREST KIN.)

ATTENTION!

Open-Call to all 'Proctor-Cook" family-members; = please submit <u>requested</u> photographs!

Edition #1

Most of the information in Edition #1 is about the Proctor-side of the family.

Edition #2

Photographs are STILL NEEDED for publication of EDITION #2. Most of the details in Edition #2 will be about the Cook-side of the family-tree. SORRY,...but please **DO NOT send unsolicited (="non-requested") photos** because they cannot be returned to you, & will be discarded.

All "requested" photos sent in by family-members, will be greatly appreciated. And given acknowledgement in the book as "credits" to the person who sends it in.

These are the "REQUESTED photos", which are needed for Edition #2 of this book:

1) Photo(s) of Robert Cook -and- his father and/or mother. 2) Photo(s) of William E. Proctor and his parents. 3) Photo(s) of Maria(h) Adams Proctor and her parents. 4) Sarah Proctor Cook, and the others of the total of thirteen (13) children of William & Maria(h) Proctor,...and...also very greatly appreciated would be a photograph of William ("Billy") Cook, the eldest, first son of Charles Wm. Cook, "Senior", and a photo of Charles "JUNIOR", the 2nd son of Charles Wm. Cook, "SENIOR" with wife, Lillian.

****

I know that the "REQUESTED Photos" are out there! **So,...PLEASE SHARE THEM!**

If you have photo(s) to submit, PLEASE CONTACT THE AUTHOR DIRECTLY at:
1-929-404-3205
Thank you!

Lexicon

Lexicon of "new words", by this author

1) <u>**Creole**</u> = (a) spelled with a capital letter-C, = a biracial person of equally-mixed, European & African race who can prove a "language-trail" back to a family's matching creolized vernacular which is based on the "mixes" of (an African language and a European language) = French, Portuguese, German (= "old- Dutch"), Spanish, or British English. (b) when spelled with a lower-case letter-c,..a creole-language is a mixture of an African-based language with one of the languages of a European-colonizer in the Americas.

2) <u>**Placage**</u> = a sort of marital-contract between a European man and a "free-woman-of-color". 3) <u>**"Obrigada"**</u> "Thank you." In Portuguese. **4) <u>Mulindian</u>** = a person who is Mulatto & Indian mixture. 5) **Blindian** = a person who is Black & Indian mixture. 6) <u>**Dougla**</u> = a person who is Black & Indian mixture in Trinidad or Guyana.

7) <u>**Blasian**</u> = a person who is Black & Asian mixture in Korea, Japan, or China.

8) <u>pleckered</u> = a mulatto, biracial, or light-skinned person who <u>**erroneously believes himself /herself to be "Black" because of the white-supremacist "one- drop-rule" invented by Walter Plecker.**</u>

9) **"Krinkly"** = textured-hair that is NOT kinky, ...but, "KRINKLY- curls", which is a thick, wild, natural mix of rough coils, blended together with soft curls.

10) <u>**"Crab-bucket"**</u> = an envious Black person who shows that he/she is racist by insisting that hybrids (= mulattos, octoroons, quadroons, and all biracial & tri- racial people) are BLACK; = "Oh just pull them into the bucket!"

11) <u>**"Crab-barrel"**</u> = an envious White or other person who shows that he/she is racist by insisting that hybrids (= mulattos, octoroons, quadroons, and all biracials & tri-racial people) are BLACK; = "Oh just push them into the barrel!"

12) "uss" = "Unified-Subjugated-Soul" = <u>**all people of the 'darker races',**</u> who have been <u>**historically systemically downtrodden**</u> by colonization, racism, and slavery.

Poem - "Deep Feelings of-a Yella-Gal"

by *Miss Utera*

Part of me is from the "slave",
part is <u>from the "Master"</u>,
Part of me is <u>"black-as- coal"</u>,
The other part is, <u>"white-as-alabaster"</u>.

****

<u>"Taxation without representation" is wrong!</u> The <u>dignity and respect</u> of a proper and <u>correct "racial identification"</u>, acknowledged by the USA government, on their forms, is due to everyone.

<u>The "WESORTS" are known to have been, during colonial times, …as the proud, "tri-racial, isolated" people of Maryland and Virginia.</u>

Since all 'mixed-race" persons are NEITHER "White", NOR "Black", …and, no matter whether he or she prefers to be called either by the appellation of Creole, Mulatto, Quadroon, Mestizo, Wesort, Coloured, "Mixed", Biracial, Tri-racial, Hybrid, Mulindian, Blindian, Blasian, Dougla, or by any other appellation;…the fact is that he/she should always be given RESPECT as a person of "mixed-race" and should be identified as such, BY LAW,… both on governmental forms, and by the general public and all citizens of this country, and internationally.

BOTTOMLINE

<u>We as one of the tri-racial groups of "mixed-race" people of America,…should be represented on governmental forms.</u>

<u>"Colorism" will end when the government gives us "mixed-race" people a box of our own to check.</u>

PETITION

Please give proper RECOGNITION & TAX-REPRESENTATION to the Tri-Racial Isolate Groups of the USA-of-America by providing them with a box to check on the next USA-FEDERAL-CENSUS of-the UNITED STATES in 2020!

A few of the historical names of the Ethnic Tri-racial Isolated, partial-Indian Groups _are:_

Wesorts,...Redbones,...Brass Ankles,...Turks,...Gouldtowners,...Moors,...Lumbees,... Jackson Whites, ...Nanticokes,...Narragansetts,...Guineas,...Portuguese,... Rappahonocks,...Chickahomonies.

(See the map on page 2 of this book for more group-names.)

Step #1:
Please sign here, as the main signature on this "petition".
X _____ Phone # _____

Then, ...

Step #2:
Collect at least five (5) other signatures as "supporters" of this cause.
(2) _____ Phone # _____
(3) _____ " _____
(4) _____ " _____
(5) _____ " _____

Step #3:
This signed "petition" will be forwarded to the Department of the Census, Washington, D.C.

****

Mail this signed "PETITION" to:
    Creole-Amerindian Genealogical Society
    P. O. Box 1268 - Cooper Station
    New York, New York 10476

About-the-Author

This author, born as _Carmelita "Carmen" Uter Cook._ is also known as <u>Carmenlita Uter</u> and/or by her legal pen-name, _"Miss Utera"._

****

<u>UTER</u> & <u>UTRA</u> are <u>Portuguese surnames</u> derived from HURTERE.

For more information about this surname, read: (1) <u>HURTERE (Utra) by Antonio Ferreira de Serpa.</u> & (2) "Grande Enciclopedia Portuguesa E Brasileira" translated from Portuguese:

<u>UTRA:</u>

A Flemish* family which passed through the island of Fayal (Azores, Portugal) in the 15th century, previously from Brussels, whose surname of origin was HURTERE*, and which is represented in Portuguese writings by the following variant spellings:

HUERTA, HUERTER, HUTER*, HUTRA*, DUTRA*, UTRA*, ULTRA, DULTRA, HUERTERE, HUTRE, URTERE*, HORTERE and UTRECHT.

According to the **rules of nomenclature in Portugal,** the **silent letter-H & the first R** were **dropped, from the surname HURTERE,** and in addition the **final E was changed to A, with the most common results being** = <u>Uter, Utra, Utrera, Utera, Urtere, D'Utra and Dutra.</u>

******

The two (2) _"nom-de-plume",_ (= pen-names), used by this author are:
Carmen Uter....................and..... "Miss Utera".
Book: "The Geechee Lady". ******* Book: "A Collection of Poems"
Book: "Miss Willa-mina". ******** *Book: "Wesort-Mulatto-Indians".

The author studied Portuguese at the University of Massachusetts-Dartmouth, and Spanish at the University of Madrid in Madrid Spain.

The author has taught in NYC schools for many years under her legal pen-name, *Miss Utera.*

Other creations of this author are:

1) Non-profit group:
Creole-American Genealogical Society, Inc.
Founded by Carmen Uter, 1983., (= dba: P.Fontaine).

....

2) **Book: 'The Geechee Lady", by Carmen Uter.**
Sub-titled: *"Grandpa's Secret Castas".*

....

3) **A Book of Poems by this author:**
"A Mulatto's Lament"; "Deep Feelings Of A Yella Gal"; by "Miss Utera".

....

4) **Book:**
Dictionary of "Five Creole Lingua-Francas", by "Miss Utera".

....

5**) "Malada Rice",** a cook-book by *"Miss Utera".* = A collection of delicious
Creole *recipes from "Grandpa's Portuguese Culinary-Arts"; 6) mixed with*
"Grandma's Geechee-style, 'low-country' ANGOLA-African cuisine.

Special Kudo: t

The '**Geechees**' of the South Carolina & Georgia Sea Islands are descendants of
ANGOLA-Africa where Portuguese is **still the official language today.**

ART

<u>**"MamzelleCreole-Collections"**</u>:

A small collection of <u>**"French-Chinoiserie"**</u> furniture, and **Asian-art** which also includes "wearable-art" (= clothing designs, tignons, <u>hair pomades</u>, and <u>facial make-up</u>) collected by this author.

7) "Translations-from-the-Portuguese", by "Miss Utera".

Bibliography

1) **"Indians of Southeast Maryland", by <u>Roundtree & Seib.</u>**

2) *<u>"The Wesorts of Southeastern Maryland", by William Harlen Gilbert.</u>*

3) **"Indivisible", edited by Gabrielle Tayac.**
    <u>(See Proctor-family information on page 115.)</u>

4) **<u>"Feast of All Saints",</u> by Anne Rice.**

5) **<u>"The Wished-For Country",</u> by Wayne Carlin.**

6) **<u>The Forgotten Portuguese, by Manuel Mira</u>**
    <u>(See "WESORTS" on page 61).</u>

7) **<u>"Name of the book: Walking Towards the Sunset,</u>**
    <u>(A Restless People, by Wayne Winkler)</u>

UTRA / UTER / UTERA/DUTRA

Family Crest

"Miss Utera"

PROCTOR-COOK FAMILY TREE

Printed in the United States
by Baker & Taylor Publisher Services